Time to Source Overseas

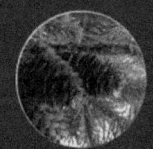

An Insiders Look at Delivering Visual Displays on Time and on Budget

••••••••••••••••••••••

Matthew Schwam

Here's What's Inside…

Introduction

March 2014
New York, NY

One of the things purchasing managers often ask me is how can we make their visual display roll-out process smoother? It seems as the world gets smaller and more and more businesses are looking to overseas to stretch their purchasing dollar further, managing the challenges of doing business overseas becomes increasingly important.

I've seen first hand the devastating effects on a roll-out when critical time-lines were overlooked in favor of creative rework and in the end the creative director was left with compromised results in stores and a purchasing manager in fear.

Most purchasing managers and creative directors are not aware of common and complex challenges we face when sourcing overseas. This book is a result of wanting to make the process of creation joyous and invigorating by creating awareness and taking the headache out of sourcing your visual displays overseas.

What follows is an interview where I share with you an insider look at the steps you can take to insure your visual display roll-out is a success...every time.

Enjoy the book!

I hope this book raises some awareness on the bigger picture and helps impact the way you look at your next visual deadline.

Warm Regards,

Matthew Schwam

Time to Source Overseas!

Susan: Good afternoon this is Susan Austin and with me today is Matthew Schwam from New York. Welcome, Matthew.

Matthew: Thank you Susan glad to be here.

Susan: Can you clarify for us the type of business you are in Matthew?

Matthew: Sure. We are a sourcing agent specializing in made to order props for visual merchandising. We utilize factories overseas in China, Taiwan and India. Sometimes other places, but those are our primary source countries. We work with visual teams domestically and internationally. We take their creative designs, turn them into mechanical drawings and place the manufacturing business with an overseas factory. Then manage the entire process, time-line and actionable events for the customer which includes producing and drop ship delivering to store locations worldwide.

Susan: Are you a middleman or is that not a term you would use?

Matthew: We are sourcing agents in the true sense of the definition. A sourcing agent provides design, factories, manufacturing expertise, quality control, freight and logistics.

Our company is in a unique partnership with our customers.

Our customer's creative directors develop and own design concepts. The concepts are tied into marketing, advertising and take visual cues from the seasons and time of year being targeted.

Our company owns the "how do we get this done" part. The first two things we do when we see a concept is create a mechanical drawing and identify factories with capabilities to produce the design. The mechanical drawing is a technical interpretation of a pretty picture aimed to walk a factory through directions on how to build. As soon as factories are qualified on the project, we bid the job and compare prototypes, pricing, timing and quality from competing factories. This ultimately leads us to the right factory to do the job. Our project managers step in and build a time and action calendared project plan with deadlines set for every actionable event. We orchestrate the project from first sample all the way to drop ship store deliveries. In our production division, we may create a project plan for up to 10 years including annual installations, removals, storage and refurbishment.

So the answer to your question "are you a middlemen" is squarely no. We are definitely strategic partners with our customers. Our core competencies are built around display manufacturing, quality sensibilities, project control, freight, logistics and installations.

In fact, we are so involved in the management of the project that our Project Managers create the deadlines (customer, company and factory) based on all of the activities required and the time that each activity takes to do it right. This is what the book is about. How to do it right. How to be successful, profitable, sustainable and get the results that we all deserve for the time, effort and passion that goes into the work.

Why Is It Advantageous to Source Overseas?

Susan: What's the advantage for a company to go overseas for their visual merchandising?

Matthew: There are many advantages to sourcing and manufacturing overseas. Among the tops are price, exclusive capabilities and options. Overseas costs can represent up to 500 percent savings compared to domestic US pricing in certain cases. The staggering advantages translate to dramatic increased purchasing power for US companies in a growing competitive environment.

As manufacturing virtually disappeared in the US in the 1960's, China and Taiwan took over in most categories. In the past 20 years, China's middle class has grown and many factory categories have exited to less developed more price competitive countries. At the same time, India's government stabilized and her economy strengthened, and so did their manufacturing capabilities. The second great advantage of manufacturing overseas is when the factory category required to produce simply does not exist in the US. In many instances, factory capabilities overseas do not exist in the US and therefore offer the sole source and only option. Examples include LED Christmas lights, injection molded and extruded nylon trees for mass production, plastic ornaments and so on. And while there are plenty of molders and fabricators in the US, they simply cannot compete on price. By that, we suggest that a US manufacturer will consistently be 25 percent more expensive on the landed cost and the premiums reach as high as 500 percent as previously mentioned.

A third unique advantage that overseas manufacturing provides is the ability to bid work to multiple qualified factories at once. This gives the buyer a competitive landscape with competing factories in multiple countries, a true international sourcing practice that ensures best quality, best price and best lead times. The interesting dynamics of bidding a design to China and India is that each country will produce the same design with specific noticeable nuances. The nuances are subjective, so there's no right or wrong. Most often, it comes down to the visual sense of the team. It's important to compare how various factories finish metal, polish crystal, finish an acrylic edge, interpret pantone colors, create hang points, develop packaging, cut foam and the list goes on and on. Point is, we need to evaluate options in order to make the best choices and boy are there plenty of options overseas.

Susan: The advantage is you get your product for a lot less. The disadvantage is the extra time and effort it takes to manage the process and transport the goods.

Matthew: Yeah, it's just not as quick or convenient as producing domestically, that's a fact. When we produce domestically, we can visit the factory and save up to a month in transit time alone.

But we pay a big financial premium for the convenience and ability to work on the shorter lead time. Most people are just not willing to do this. So time becomes the premium trading card. The more you have, the more likely we can run an overseas manufacturing process with a high probability of success while saving a lot of money and delivering extraordinary value.

Why Doing Business Overseas Can Be Problematic...

Susan: Do you think sourcing things overseas is problematic by nature?

Matthew: The big success driver for sourcing overseas is a thorough thoughtful time-line with actionable events, accurate milestones, participants willing and able to work under the kind of rigid structure this type of business needs and time to execute. When everyone aligns and commits to the deadlines, great results are the natural bi-product. When there are problems, it's usually when people are ignoring time-lines. Which as we alluded to, are more critical due to the extra time required doing business overseas.

Success is in the Details...

Susan: In your experience, what are some of the things that get in the way of someone having a successful display roll-out? What would be a reason it wouldn't go well?

Matthew: Our customers are usually starting with a concept, trying to explore a look and feel before committing to specific designs, dimensions, colors and specifications. They may have a general idea of what they want, but they haven't fully dialed it in yet. Typical of how most creative people set an idea in motion.

I understand it mostly because it is the process that I follow. In my companies, I am the CEO, but I am also the Creative Director. If someone does not tell me time to stop, I will go forever, seeing something new each time I revisit a creation. I experience designing as a process and when I'm engaged, it's a process that I never want to end. It's the zone. The space where I feel most like myself. Knowing that I can personally be an infinite creator has forced me to surround myself with finite business thinkers, numbers guys and project managers. In my very nature I think limitlessly and see possibilities that most don't see. I see the future which allows me to take risk with ease and confidence. I intuitively know quality. When I revisit a design concept, I see new and more interesting possibilities that were not apparent during the previous session. I see life as a process of advancing my awareness and at each level, life, the people in it and the objects look new and sometimes as if I am seeing them for the first time. I am forgiving to myself and to others and this translates to an ability to create blank pages and start new chapters when the storyline is not in sync with my spirit. There is no beginning and no end for me. There is right here, right now and my desire to realize the highest and best purpose for this moment.

Without a thoughtful caring and understanding team around me, I would stay in exploration mode indefinitely, always looking for new insight. While in so many ways these traits have proven to be great assets to my life, I had to learn to surround myself with a structured team. Prior to building my team, I was the root cause of beautiful, organized, chaotic, ongoing, indecisive and creative behaviors. We were not able to continue to run our business this way. The solution was born in my awareness of my nature and recognition of the balance that was required to run my business as a world class operation. Now, I keep myself in my core competency sweet spot while still managing all of the other priorities of the company with people operating in their respective core competencies.

The challenge is that the manufacturing process requires exacting specificity. The very specifications that do not exist in the designers world when in concept phase. Concept phase is when a designer wants to know all options. But the purchasing and project managers require specificity if the factory is expected to produce a sample that the creative team can be passionate for.

We have gotten good at filling in blanks and developing missing details in order to get the ball rolling and produce working samples. We do this with pleasure and on occasion develop solutions that stick. But more often than not, the first samples trigger a series of thoughts from creative that start to mold the design. Since time is the great commodity and samples can take up to 10 days or more to produce, clarity and decisiveness are critical to successful overseas sourcing.

The great teams show up ready to go, with all the details required for a factory to build an accurate prototype. We understand not every team has the resources to provide that kind of information so a lot of times we are vetting out those details. Until we get them we can't really provide an accurate response. Lack of detail can eat up valuable time getting a project off the ground that would be so much more useful to use for much needed contingency time during the production run.

Susan: They have a concept but there's no real depth to the concept; it's just an idea at this stage and so it's hard for you to then give them what they need to make it happen. Interesting.

Matthew: It's pretty typical for creative people to think in concept long before considering a single detail. The details really don't matter if the concept fails to pass stage one. Notwithstanding, the best creatives have support teams that treat each and every concept as if it will survive, creating conceptual details upfront that are based on a series of what ifs. The approach takes more time to plan, but when the concept lands, the team is rewarded with a 10-20 day head start on the full development of the landed concept. It's huge in our world of deadlines, high stakes selling seasons and critical in store dates coordinated around a well orchestrated symphony of television campaigns, print ads, radio, publicity stunts and merchandise launches. We need to understand the concept but we need granular detail to produce a successful result and save valuable time later.

It's the same hard easy theory that applies to all parts of life. Hard work upfront produces an easy flow later. Easy flow upfront produces hard work later. It's tempting to be lazy upfront and leave out the what ifs because most concepts die on the vine. But when the concept survives, the project did not start right. And once the project is set in motion, it's difficult to return to previously short-cutted steps and start over. It's like pouring a bad foundation and trying to build a skyscraper. And when there is no time to go back and pour it right, the structure is shaky before the first piece of steel is installed. As soon as the design is locked and development starts, the clock starts ticking against the fixed delivery date. Every day spent on vetting out details is a direct debit from production and transit days required to insure great results. Best practice on this is to treat every concept as if it will be the final selection. Start the way we want to finish. Touch it once.

Susan: If the creative has the concept, is there someone else on the customer team that's responsible for the detail?

Matthew: The typical structure is a creative team lead by a creative director and a purchasing team headed by the purchasing manager. It's the purchasing manager's responsibility internally to collect and capture the granular detail and provide it to the team.

Susan: And the work you do is unique to each order right?

Matthew: The core competency of our company is fabricating custom made to order design. Our depth of expertise with a comprehensive variety of materials sets us apart. We manufacture with all materials placing us in a position to successfully source most designs that land. We have the team and the factories to perform at the highest level. We understand the critical path to get the results. As long as we have the time, we get everything we set out for and more.

The Paradox of Creative Tension...

Susan: The creative comes up with the concept, why is the purchasing team then not able to give you those details you need? What's the roadblock?

Matthew: In my experience, most creative directors don't want to get bogged down in details in the beginning. They want to explore all options, all concepts and all possibilities. Creative directors have a very hard time finishing and stamping a drawing and saying the words "We're done, this is perfect." They are always striving for bigger and better.

Creative people are explorers, dreamers, risk takers. They are visionaries living in a world of infinite possibilities, optimistic and always ready to take on a challenge.

It's a very different profile to that of a purchasing manager. The purchasing manager is creative's strategic partner to make sure the vision gets executed at the highest level, with specificity, on time and on budget. The typical purchasing manager is a down and dirty, all business, nuts and bolts, time and action person. They like excel spreadsheets, and desire deadlines. Effectively, their job is to delivery what creative has promised.

It's a very interesting dynamic. It's part of the joy of being in the business. But this dichotomy is really central to the timing challenges that retail teams face all over the country.

The very natures of creative and purchasing personalities are opposite which technically makes a perfectly balanced team. That is, if they understand, appreciate and respect each other's roles goals and objectives in the process.

Understanding What's at Stake...

Susan: You have two very unique personality types at work here. The creative team is probably a very different group of individuals than the purchasing team. Is there a way to get them on the same page from the start or is that just a fantasy and it's never going to happen?

Matthew: You can definitely get them on the same page but it requires everyone to really understand what everyone else's challenges are. Sometimes we get self absorbed into our own challenges and we really forget about, disregard or lack sensitivity to other team members. My company is set up as a mirror image of our customers; we've got a creative team, sourcing managers, project managers, purchasing managers, factory partners, freight and logistics experts and everybody has their own set up responsibilities. Notwithstanding, interdependency is central to the success of the team.

If you think about it, the world is so completely interdependent with our daily needs for commodities, currency, culture, communication, politics and spirituality. When we are in sync on these topics with our neighbors, we have peace. When we are out of sync, we have conflict. Same thing applies to the business team. In sync, peace. Out of sync, conflict. When we start a new project we get everyone on the same page with real time project management transparency. Total team buy-in is the only way to achieve an in sync successful outcome.

Visibility to tasks, milestones and deadlines is a great way for people to understand the challenges of the interdependent team. The interdependent team results in members acting thoughtfully with everyone else's goals in mind while they simultaneously manage their own priorities and deadlines. If we can help teams work interdependently by shining a light on the challenges that each member faces, the team will turn stronger, results will improve and the companies that we are hired to support will be more profitable.

Susan: Shining that light is the reason for this book right? You want to educate your clients what the challenges are and how change in mindset will save time and money. Can you share with us some of the things that go wrong when deadlines are missed? What's the reality of that?

Matthew: The worst thing that happens is when the timing of the team is out of sync with the timing of factory production, ocean freight and distribution. What normally happens is the factory produces the product, puts it on a boat, we bring it to a distribution center, we put it on a truck and then it gets deliver to the store locations.

Those three activities each come with a finite number of days to complete including insurance days to manage the known but elusive time factors required for contingency to be discussed in the next paragraph. So the minimum time requirements are fixed and unmovable. When the client is delayed in producing a purchase order and critical required days are lost, then something has to give.

There are common challenges that come along with manufacturing overseas that people don't know too much about. As a responsible experienced partner, we build contingency days into each critical stage of the process to mitigate. We think of these contingency days as insurance, hence the name of the book. We purchase insurance because stuff happens. The tricky thing is that none of us can predict when it's going to happen. So we purchase the insurance and most often, we don't use it. But statistically, we all know that stuff happens, and it will, at some point. So we always need to have coverage.

If we think about the extra days built into a time and action as insurance, we will gain a new appreciation for the importance of the project plan and all the critical deadlines attached.

Common issues include raw material defects, machine malfunctions, human error, customs delays, acts of God such as typhoons, monsoons, hurricanes, snow and so on.

Consider how a purchase order issued 10 days past deadline can compromise a job when a common challenge occurs and 10 days of insurance is all we would have needed to solve it. When the extra days are no longer available, the most common option is to make up time by expediting freight. This is an option that may get the product in store on time but at a cost. Either additional funds are provided to pay the freight. Or a part of the budget is reallocated from product to freight. Please see Appendix A: Budget Loss Analysis.

Susan: All this stemming from not having the project parameters from the start and as a result you have to make stuff up, play catch up and give up insurance days built in for common challenges.

Matthew: There is no catch up required when teams show up to the game ready to play. If the coach shows up to game day with his team but no game plan, the team is at a disadvantage before the game even starts. When basic data is not available to the interdependent team, some members are at a distinct disadvantage, unable to do their jobs to the fullest and the giant liability is that the precious commodity time is wasted. Please see Appendix: Typical Time and Action.

Susan: You're in kind of a tricky position if I'm understanding you correctly because the creative director that doesn't want to get bogged down in the details is ultimately your client, and so is the purchasing manager.

Matthew: It's a very difficult position. We are appreciative when we are selected to develop a project, so the last thing we want to do is complain. But we also have an obligation to provide information, deadlines and a time-line that we know are required to produce the project on time, on budget and at the quality level that we need. So, what do we do when that advice is not taken?

Susan: Right.

Overseas Sourcing Can Be Successful for All Types of Businesses...

Susan: Do you find this problem is mostly for companies who are new to overseas sourcing? Or is it because these projects are so unique they sometimes take on a life of their own?

Matthew: Most of our customers have been doing this for a long time, they are experienced and they understand exactly what it takes to get it done. But the decision makers are often working in bureaucratic organizations that sometimes prohibit them from moving forward at the pace that the individuals know is required. We have customers whose corporate time-line is completely in sync with overseas sourcing so this doesn't apply to everyone. For those who know, but cannot take action, it might be that changing the rhythm of the time-lines may be too big a task to accomplish with the small teams that are in place. With scaled down teams they might just not be able to catch up to get themselves working far enough in advance.

Susan: Are you saying that some companies have to go through layers of approval and it may just be the way their approval system internally is setup that they are not always able to respond to required time-lines. Sounds like some of the customers haven't made the shift from the 1960's mentality of manufacturing here in the US to going overseas. Do you think they are still working on domestic time-lines even though they are squarely manufacturing in China, Taiwan and India?

Matthew: That's interesting. Come to think of it, most of corporate printing still happens here in the US. And lead times are very short for print. And of course the creative and purchasing approach to print is wait to the end so that printed material is always as closely aligned as possible with the most current marketing message. We see marketing messages evolve quickly as they respond to fast paced economic conditions, retail landscape, financial results, social climate and other factors. So it is largely a goal to wait as long as possible to print collateral material that reflects the most current real time message.

The present print time line is very similar to the old domestic manufacturing time-line. Wait as long as you can to keep marketing, advertising and in store messaging in sync, then go to press. The new paradigm of manufacturing overseas, however, forces teams to forecast several months in advance. Waiting for same quarter cues from marketing and advertising is a thing of the past. Maybe the question worth asking is if the current print time-line and the old 1960's domestic time-line are interfering with the new required overseas time-line. They are very different.

The teams that really have it together are writing purchase orders 5 to 6 months out in front of in store delivery dates. So, they'll start conceptualizing and prototyping 10 to 12 months out for a big roll-out. That's the ideal situation and the 10 to 12 month time-line sets the condition for success. The success happens very consistently when teams are in sync with planning and preparation. So the challenge is how do you get everyone on board with that time-line?

Susan: Maybe not understanding the true ramifications of what happens if they aren't on board with the deadline or the importance of a deadline.

Matthew: I will tell you, if you are not on board with the time-line and the process proceeds late, money is the penalty in one form or another.

The Roll-Out Parameters
Needed for Success...

Susan: Let's talk about what they need to understand, Matthew for a successful roll-out, what are the roll-out parameters? What do they need to know or understand for this to be a success?

Matthew: We need to know how much time is required to produce. Timing is something that we find out very quickly. Once we deliver the details of the product to our factory including dimensions, pantone colors, mechanical drawings, quantities and deadlines we know within three days how long the factory needs to produce from the day they receive a purchase order. So, there are probably three critical timing points that are important to know from there; 1. how long does the factory need to procure and produce, 2. how long will it take to get to the US by sea and 3. how long will it take to distribute domestic to store locations.

So understanding those dates is equivalent to defining the deadline for decision-making, which in our world is the purchase order deadline. That's really all you need to understand. How long does the factory need? How long does it take to transport it from overseas to here? How long does it take to distribute domestically? Once we deliver those dates it's a race to the purchase order and figuring out all the things that have to happen internally for all stakeholders to be positioned for decision making.

The Proof Is in the Parameters…

Susan: So it sounds like from what you just described, knowing these critical dates isn't enough is it? You're saying sometimes, it's not that they are ignoring them, but they are immune to them for various reasons, organization bureaucracy being one of them.

Matthew: Yeah. There's some truth in that, Susan..

Susan: Well, maybe what's missing is the buy-in? There is a gap. There's definitely some kind of missing link in the chain. Do you think if an international mindset was adapted, would that solve the challenge?

Matthew: Yes.

Susan: I assume the in-store dates are set in stone. If something goes sideways and there is no insurance time to fix it, deliveries can be missed, right?

We Can't Move Christmas...

Matthew: That's right. The first days of spring, summer and fall are already on the calendar from here to eternity. Christmas happens on the same day every year.

Susan: Yeah, you can't move Christmas.

Matthew: If you miss your date, you disconnect with your merchandising initiative, advertising and marketing campaigns. It could really punish the company in a very competitive retail environment.

Susan: Yeah, and I would imagine if that happens, as you alluded to earlier, jobs are at risk. This is the company brand at stake, too.

Matthew: If an international overseas time-line were adapted into corporate America, it would greatly benefit many of our customers. It's like an anti-print approach.

Here's What Happens When Deadlines Get Missed...

Susan: Lets dig into this a little further. What happens when deadlines start to get missed Matthew?

Matthew: Based on initial quotes and project timelines, everyone can see in black and white how much product will be purchased for the budget. The day you miss your first deadline, you are probably paying for something that you weren't planning for before you missed the deadline. As soon as you start spending money on things that don't add value to the end goal, the companies procurement objectives are diluted and devalued.

Susan: Right. There are only so many ways to cut the pie, unless the pie is willing to get bigger and it probably isn't, then something has to be compromised.

Matthew: Yeah, correct. I mean, a lot of people give up product because they are all of a sudden paying for expedited freight, overtime and/or new necessary services. So that's probably the biggest thing people need to know.

Here's Where We Add Value...

Susan: It's your customer, too. This isn't a vendor that you can beat up on; it's the other way around.

Matthew: We are just a strategic instrument in this process using our manufacturing and logistics expertise, which is where we're needed. That's where we add value. We don't ever feel like we are being beat up on. We just need the market to understand the complexities in the work that we do in order to yield successful results, without the gambles.

Here's the Project Parameters for a Successful Roll-Out...

Susan: What are some of the project parameters, Matthew, that you would like to see handled before you get to the PO stage?

Matthew: For a successful roll out we need detailed a delivery date, a distribution list, artwork, mechanical drawings, pantone colors, dimensions, budgets, total quantities, quantities per inner and outer carton and as much context for how and where product will be used in store.

Freight Challenges...

Susan: Could you explain how international shipment works?

Matthew: We are shipping product cubes in containers. There is a financial priority to create the most efficient smallest cube per product unit to deliver the maximum number of units on each container. We balance this financial priority with the practical priority of delivering product to the store that is easy to understand and install. Space on vessels is carefully coordinated with our production schedules. Exit factory dates and transit time from factory to port are planned to meet the vessel cutoff date. Most often containers that originate in China and Taiwan deliver to our West Coast distribution center. India containers generally move to our port Newark center. International shipments move direct from the origin factory to distribution centers in Europe and Asia. Each item requires specific customs coding and certifications to move from one country to another. There are lots of logistics involved in moving freight. We've got to schedule those containers, make sure there is enough room for our product on the freight liners and it all has to be scheduled well in advance to meet or beat vessel cutoff dates at each port. We've got a very competent team of people on our end who coordinate all of the details.

Common challenges that can delay freight include securing vessel space, meeting vessel cutoff times, extreme weather conditions, inter-country transportation and customs inspections.

Factory Challenges...

Susan: Could you explain how the factory process works?

Matthew: There's no topic that a factory cannot fix. But contingency time is required. The issues that factories face include raw material lead times, raw material defects, raw material shortages, raw material that is not delivered to spec, machine failure, human failure, quality control, weather conditions, space limitations, yield miscalculations, and so on.

Each factory has their own specific core competencies. The objects that go into production that are not core competencies are outsourced. A factory whose producing a car doesn't have every nut, bolt and can of paint sitting in their facility ready to produce the car at the time of the PO. If a link of the chain breaks, it could reek havoc on the factory time-line for final production.

We know that things are going to happen, we just don't know when. So, the smart game is to see the spectrum of possibilities, evaluate averages and probabilities and provide insurance in units of measure of 24 hour days to mitigate the risk; that simple.

If a machine yielding 1000 units a day breaks down, you're losing output fast until it's fixed. If a factory has contingency days built in nobody is affected and life goes on.

But, if they had to give those days away to a late purchase order they might have a problem that starts a ripple affect straight down the process line.

Connect the dots...

Susan: Can you share insights on the cause and effects factors of the time-line?

Matthew: While the time-line has many parallel path activities, it is linear and dependent by nature. In other words, the time-line is mostly a series of steps that happen in order where one step cannot start until the previous step is complete. There are a series of hand-offs.

Here's a simplified look at that.

Step 1: Concept

Step 2: Mechanical drawing

Step 3: Factory sample

Step 4: Quantities, Pack-outs, Delivery dates, Budgets, Specifications

Step 5: Accurate pricing

Step 6: Purchase order

Step 7: Factory raw material purchase

Step 8: Manufacture

Step 8: QC

Step 9: Exit factory

Step 10: Factory to port

Step 11: Port to port

Step 12:   Customs clear

Step 13: Port to DC

Step 14: DC to store

The process is a series of linear dependencies which highlights the importance of providing each step with the proper time and detail to complete its part, on time and accurate. You can imagine how one missed deadline can trickle fast and furious throughout the balance of the process affecting everything in its path. When things go wrong, the freight, being at the end of the process is the last date to get hit and may or may not have time to recover. I have seen first hand that thoughtful planning and preparation is the key ingredient to preventing having to confront the liabilities of overseas sourcing.

More Examples of What Can Go Wrong with Overseas Sourcing...

Susan: Can you give us another example?

Matthew: I hate to keep harping Susan. And please don't get me wrong; this is not a book about fear, doubt and worry. To the contrary, we are talking about awareness, preparation and planning. So being eyes wide open aware, thoughtful and proactive is the message. Knowledge is empowering and when we are empowered, we are in sync with the universe and when that happens, we flow like water. I want our customer jobs to flow like water.

Having said that, weather is another factor, no pun intended. There's a rainy season which yields a lot of humidity. When we have handmade product that needs dry time, humidity is a factor. We plan for humidity based on history and forecasts in context with time of year. It's another real factor that might not happen but if it does, better have insurance.

It's probably the kind of stuff that nobody wants to be involved with but they need to know about. As the strategic manufacturing partner, we are responsible for managing the liability complexities, but the interdependent nature of our relationship with customers requires awareness and partnership on the topic. Because I think the mentality is often "If you want our business, you'll figure out how to get it done quicker." Right? "If you want to do business with us, you'll negotiate with the factory. We know they have contingency time. They can make this happen."

I hope that it is evident by now that there are extra insurance days planted at every stage of the process. And insurance should never be compromised or negotiated with so much at stake.

How Removing Contingencies Exposes You to Unacceptable Risk...

Susan: It's an interesting dynamic going on here. As you point out, the client is putting themselves at great risk when they do not comply with the time-lines.

Matthew: When I was starting out in my first business, I went for five years with no health insurance. I was so concerned about stretching the investment money I had into the business that I inadvertently risked the company itself. I convinced myself that I was invincible, unable to get sick or injured. Had I had any type of hospitalization that lasted for more than a few days, it would have wiped out all the money that I made in real estate that was being used to finance my new business. The insurance money that I saved would have represented a tiny fraction of what I would have spent if something that happens to people would have happened to me. I got lucky. Not even a doctor's visit in those days. Not a single medical expense in the 5 year period that I was without health insurance. But in retrospect, it was crazy. To think that I could have lost the very thing that I was trying so hard to build and protect is frightening in retrospect.

We have the right to be optimistic about our business process, but we also have an obligation to share the risks of overseas manufacturing. The cost benefits of manufacturing overseas compared to domestic manufacturing are obvious. But there are many more considerations and moving parts doing business overseas. This is not a problem, just an observation that needs to be recognized if we want to raise awareness and be successful. So anticipation is the name of the game. If I had been a bit wiser back in 1995 when I started my first company, I would have anticipated some type of injury that would have required medical attention and big bills. And then I would have made the speculative investment for health insurance.

We need to be prudent with each other and transparent with risk reward profiles. In our business, there is a standard practice of presenting a time-line with specific dates, actions and milestones from beginning to end for every development. Every step of our process gets a specific required number of days to complete.

We recently invested in real time, transparent Project Management software for all team members to be on the same time-line. We call it PMImage. The gold standard starts the process providing all team members visibility to time and action.

Susan: If you had the time, can you really fix all of these issues when they happen?

Matthew: We have spent 10 years building a world class team of people who each are the best in their area of expertise. Each uniquely qualified to solve any challenge that comes their way. There is no challenge our team cannot solve as long as the time-lines are not compromised.

Our customers often feel "Why give all the extra days to common challenges that might not happen?" In our business, there is usually no value to being early. So the thought process is that just in time is just fine. But we have seen the problems and expenses incurred later when insurance days were given away due to missed deadlines. The cost upfront might not ultimately have been necessary. But when there is a problem, the speculative investment made is significantly less than the premium costs of solving the problem in real time.

Susan: Sounds like the peace of mind that comes with having the insurance, in your case, adhering to the time-line would be well worth it. I can see now how doing business overseas can be such an advantage, but I also see that there needs to be a shift in how most teams plan, prepare and move through the process.

Here's How to Ensure Your Next Roll-Out Will Be a Success...

Susan: For those that are wanting more information from you for how can they work with you, what are the next steps?

Matthew: Next steps are usually a face-to-face meeting where we discuss the project parameters. With PMImage we can get your next project started and help you understand what each and every step is, what the tasks are and the timing associated. Of course, we will add big value delivering quality factories to produce best in class product, this is what we are known for.

Susan: How can people reach you to get started?

Matthew: They can reach me at: mschwam@holidayimageinc.com or mschwam@retailimage.com.

Susan: Thanks Matthew this has been very enlightening. Companies should take note.

Matthew: Thanks Susan. We have the same goal as our clients: We want their overseas sourcing to be a big win for them. They can get the product they want on time and on budget! And hopefully we've shined a light on the subject of overseas sourcing and the importance of time.

Appendix

Sample Time Line

Budget Loss Analysis Spreadsheet

	Projected Effective Days
	China
DOMESTIC FREIGHT OPTIONS	
Domestic Ground	7
Domestic 3 Day	5
Domestic 2 Day	4
Domestic Air	3
DOMESTIC DISTRIBUTION	
6 Day Service	8
OVERSEAS FREIGHT OPTIONS	
Port Arrival, Air, Offload, Customs Clearance	7
Port Arrival, Ocean, Offload, Customs Clearance	21
TRANSIT TO PORT from factory exit	2
Total Transit Time from factory exit to store	
Ocean/Domestic Ground	38
Ocean/Domestic 3 Day	36
Ocean/Domestic 2 Day	35
Ocean/Domestic Air	34
Air/Domestic Ground	24
Air/Domestic 3 Day	22
Air/Domestic 2 Day	21
Air/Domestic Air	20

Budget Loss Analysis
PO Deadline based on 11/1 in store
Price for Prop Item : 48" x 24" x24" (Vol Wt : 167 lbs) Price / Unit : $500.00
Budget of $ 250,000 for purchase

china

Factory Lead Time	Total Days	PO Date for 11/1 Delivery	OCEAN FREIGHT(16 CUFT) FedEx Ground Service	Store Delivered Price	# of Units in Budget	Loss (%)
90	128	26/06/2012	$222.08	$722.08	346	0.00%
75	113	11/07/2012	$222.08	$722.08	346	0.00%
60	98	26/07/2012	$222.08	$722.08	346	0.00%
45	83	10/08/2012	$222.08	$722.08	346	0.00%
30	68	25/08/2012	$222.08	$722.08	346	0.00%

Factory Lead Time	Total Days	PO Date for 11/1 Delivery	OCEAN/FedEx 3 DAY	Store Delivered Price	# of Units in Budget	Loss (%)
90	126	28/06/2012	$681.82	$1,181.82	212	38.73%
75	111	13/07/2012	$681.82	$1,181.82	212	38.73%
60	96	28/07/2012	$681.82	$1,181.82	212	38.73%
45	81	12/08/2012	$681.82	$1,181.82	212	38.73%
30	66	27/08/2012	$681.82	$1,181.82	212	38.73%

Factory Lead Time	Total Days	PO Date for 11/1 Delivery	OCEAN/FEDEX 2 DAY	Store Delivered Price	# of Units in Budget	Loss (%)
90	125	29/06/2012	$1,048.95	$1,548.95	161	53.46%
75	110	14/07/2012	$1,048.95	$1,548.95	161	53.46%
60	95	29/07/2012	$1,048.95	$1,548.95	161	53.46%
45	80	13/08/2012	$1,048.95	$1,548.95	161	53.46%
30	65	28/08/2012	$1,048.95	$1,548.95	161	53.46%

Factory Lead Time	Total Days	PO Date for 11/1 Delivery	OCEAN/FEDEX NEXT DAY	Store Delivered Price	# of Units in Budget	Loss (%)
90	124	30/06/2012	$1,190.45	$1,690.45	148	56.73%
75	109	15/07/2012	$1,190.45	$1,690.45	148	56.73%
60	94	30/07/2012	$1,190.45	$1,690.45	148	56.73%
45	79	14/08/2012	$1,190.45	$1,690.45	148	56.73%
30	64	29/08/2012	$1,190.45	$1,690.45	148	56.73%

Factory Lead Time	Total Days	PO Date for 11/1 Delivery	16 CUFT=167 LBS/AIR+FEDEX GRN	Store Delivered Price	# of Units in Budget	Loss (%)
90	114	10/07/2012	$470.11	$970.11	258	25.43%
75	99	25/07/2012	$470.11	$970.11	258	25.43%
60	84	09/05/2012	$470.11	$970.11	258	25.43%
45	69	24/05/2012	$470.11	$970.11	258	25.43%
30	54	08/08/2012	$470.11	$970.11	258	25.43%

Factory Lead Time	Total Days	PO Date for 11/1 Delivery	AIR+FEDEX 3 DAYS	Store Delivered Price	# of Units in Budget	Loss (%)
90	112	12/07/2012	$929.85	$1,429.85	175	49.42%
75	97	27/07/2012	$929.85	$1,429.85	175	49.42%
60	82	11/08/2012	$929.85	$1,429.85	175	49.42%
45	67	26/08/2012	$929.85	$1,429.85	175	49.42%
30	52	10/08/2012	$929.85	$1,429.85	175	49.42%

Factory Lead Time	Total Days	PO Date for 11/1 Delivery	AIR+FEDEX 2 DAYS	Store Delivered Price	# of Units in Budget	Loss (%)
90	111	11/07/2012	$1,296.98	$1,796.98	139	59.83%
75	96	28/07/2012	$1,296.98	$1,796.98	139	59.83%
60	81	12/08/2012	$1,296.98	$1,796.98	139	59.83%
45	66	27/08/2012	$1,296.98	$1,796.98	139	59.83%
30	51	11/08/2012	$1,296.98	$1,796.98	139	59.83%

Factory Lead Time	Total Days	PO Date for 11/1 Delivery	AIR+FEDEX NEXT DAY	Store Delivered Price	# of Units in Budget	Loss (%)
90	110	12/07/2012	$1,438.48	$1,938.48	129	62.71%
75	95	29/07/2012	$1,438.48	$1,938.48	129	62.71%
60	80	13/08/2012	$1,438.48	$1,938.48	129	62.71%
45	65	28/08/2012	$1,438.48	$1,938.48	129	62.71%
30	50	12/08/2012	$1,438.48	$1,938.48	129	62.71%

NOTE: FedEx Rates based on 2012 Published rates before Discount

Abbreviated Time and Action

May
           1st Kick-off.

           7th Samples and technical drawings to   factories.

         17th First Sample Reviewed.

         25th Second Sample reviewed.

         26th Second Sample Approved.

         28th Meeting:

Agenda

A. Review final pricing.

B. Review pre-production samples.

C. Review QC process.

D. Review distribution list.

E. Verify case packs.

F. Confirm critical dates.

G. Schedule regular follow up calls/meetings.

June
         1st Purchase Order to HI.

        15th QC.

        19th Production samples.

July
        15th QC inline.

August
        5th Final QC.

        15th Factory exit.

September   **4th** **Port Arrival.**

        7th DC arrival.

        21st DC exit.

Acknowledgements

Thank you to so many of you who have supported our business since 2004.

American Eagle, American Express, Ann Taylor, AT&T, Barneys, Bebe, Bergdorf Goodman, Body Shop, Bose, DKNY, Durst Organization, Dillard's, Fortunoff, Gap, General Growth Properties, Guess, Gymboree, Harry Rosen, Hearst, H&M, HJ Kalikow, Hugo Breitling, Brookfield Properties, Burberry, Cache, Carter's, Cartier, CBRE, Coach, Cole Haan, Colliers, DeBeers Boss, HUMC, Intercontinental Hotels, J Crew, Jack and Janie, Johnson & Murphy, L Brands, La Senza, Lord and Taylor, Macy's, Mandarin Oriental, Neiman Marcus, North Face, Oxford Properties, Peninsula Hotel, Pink, Polo Ralph Lauren, Related Companies, Saks Fifth Avenue, Sephora, Silverstein Properties, St John, Tiffany, Tishman Speyer Properties, Tourneau, Tumi, Under Armour, Victoria's Secret, Vince, Vornado Realty Trust, White House Black Market, Zales, Jillian, Gavin, Grace, Griffin ☺

Author Biography

Matthew Schwam is a 19 year veteran of sourcing overseas, having starting his first business in 1995 importing and re purposing African art into contemporary furniture.

Matthew started Holiday Image in 2004 to source and manufacture seasonal display props for retail environments. The Holiday Image production division develops a branded design approach for office lobby portfolios and hotels with holiday decor.

Retail Image is launching March, 2014 to design, source and manufacture custom wood and metal store fixtures, carpet and decoratives for retail environments.

Gavin Matthews will launch in April, 2014 to design, source and manufacture made to order wood and metal furniture for designers and architects focused on hotel developments and high end residential design.

Matthew graduated from Boston University School of Management 1990 and lives in Tribeca, New York with his wife Jillian and 3 children: Gavin, Grace and Griffin.

Matthew grew up in a family display business where his childhood and teenage years were spent working in design, shipping, receiving, sourcing and installation departments of the company.

During his first 6 years of career in commercial real estate in NYC, he was mentored by some of the brightest entrepreneurs in the world where he was advised to follow his passions for business, design and manufacturing, which is how he ended up where he is today. His management core competency is in placing passionate people where their unique abilities fit best to nurture their own spirits and ultimately the best interests of Holiday Image, Retail Image and Gavin Matthews.

His personal passions and unique abilities are in design, architecture, quality materials and manufacturing.

Here is how to insure your visual display roll-out is delivered on time and on budget.

You already know how important handling your overseas visual display roll-out is. Keeping the creative director happy but coming in on budget and on time involves a lot of moving parts and involves coordinating a lot of different and often conflicting priorities.

That's where we come in. We help people just like you get their visual display in store, on budget and with a happy creative director.

Step 1: We meet with you to discuss your projects vision and parameters and share with you our Image Project Manager to use.

Step 2: We help you identify the key milestones that must be adhered to keep your roll-out on track and to ensure your roll-out stays insured.

Step 3: We take it from here and coordinate all the moving pieces and parts to get your visual display roll-out developed, sourced and delivered.

Now you can get your visual display roll-out project started off the right way and ensure you are the project hero.

If you'd like us to help, just send an email to: MSCHWAM@HOLIDAYIMAGEINC.COM and we will take it from there.

Please visit:
www.holidayimageinc.com, www.retailimage.com or
www.gavinmatthewsllc.com and request your own
copy of PMImage.